On the Move
IN WORDS AND PICTURES

Ruth Thomson

Watts Books
London • New York • Sydney

You have to push to make these go.

tricycle

skateboard

roller skates

scooter

unicycle

mountain bike

racing bike

tandem

Some animals can be used for transport.

horse

camel

donkey

elephant

pony trap

ox cart

horse and dray

horse carriage

How many of these do you see every day?

motor scooter

motorbike

van

car

pick-up truck

lorry

camper

delivery van

These vehicles carry paying passengers.

bus

coach

tram

double-decker bus

rickshaw

school bus

taxi

underground train

These vehicles carry heavy loads.

petrol tanker

car transporter

logging truck

refrigerated lorry

dump truck

removal van

milk tanker

container lorry

Where do you see these?

tractor

combine harvester

street sweeper

dust cart

mobile crane

digger

tow truck

snowplough

Trains travel along rails.

steam train

diesel train

electric train

bullet train

monorail

rack railway

freight train

double-decker train

People have fun on the water with these.

rowing boat

canoe

sailboard

kayak

dinghy

yacht

catamaran

speedboat

These working boats travel across the sea.

ferry

dhow

junk

fishing boat

ocean liner

oil tanker

container ship

freighter

Have you ever travelled up in the air?

hang glider

glider

hot air balloon

airship

helicopter

light aircraft

Jumbo jet

Concorde

Have you ever seen any of these?

cable car

dune buggy

hovercraft

gondola

racing car

skidoo

sand yacht

go-kart

© 1993 Watts Books

Watts Books
96 Leonard Street
London EC2A 4RH

Franklin Watts Australia
14 Mars Road
Lane Cove
NSW 2066

UK ISBN: 0 7496 1136 7

Dewey Decimal Classification 388

10 9 8 7 6 5 4 3 2 1

A CIP catalogue record for this book
is available from the British Library

Photographs: B & C Alexander 16 (br), 23 (tr); Aviation Picture
Library 7 (tl, bl), 11 (br), 20 (tr, br), 21 (all); DLP Photo Library 6 (tr),
12 (bl); Eye Ubiquitous 4 (tl), 5 (tr), 7 (br), 8 (bl), 12 (tl, tr, br), 15 (tl),
17 (tl), 18 (tl), 19 (bl), 20 (tl), 22 (tl), 23 (tl); Chris Fairclough Colour
Library 2 (tl), 3 (bl), 4 (tr, bl), 5 (bl, br), 8 (tl), 10 (tl), 11 (bl), 13 (tl, tr),
15 (bl), 16 (bl), 22 (br); Robert Harding Picture Library 4 (br), 9 (bl),
15 (tr); Peter Millard cover (bl), 3 (tl, br); Andrew Morland 9 (tl),
18 (tr), 22 (tr), 23 (bl); Quadrant Picture Library 6 (tl, bl, br), 7 (tr),
8 (tr), 9 (tr), 10 (tr, bl), 11 (tl), 13 (bl, br), 14 (tl, tr, bl), 15 (br), 17 (br),
19 (br); Watts Books/Chris Fairclough cover (tr), 2 (tr, bl), 3 (tr),
10 (br); ZEFA cover (tl, br), 2 (br), 5 (tl), 8 (br), 9 (br), 11 (tr), 14 (br),
16 (tl, tr), 17 (tr, bl), 18 (bl, br), 19 (tl, tr), 22 (bl), 23 (br).

Printed in Malaysia